Teachers Are Terrific!

Artwork by Lila Rose Kennedy

HARVEST HOUSE PUBLISHERS
Eugene, Oregon

Teachers Are Terrific!

Text Copyright © 2000 Harvest House Publishers
Eugene, Oregon 97402

ISBN 0-7369-0386-0

Artwork designs are reproduced under license from © Arts Uniq'®, Inc., Cookeville, TN and may not be reproduced without permission. For information regarding art prints featured in this book, please contact:

Arts Uniq'
P.O. Box 3085
Cookeville, TN 38502
800-223-5020

Design and production by Garborg Design Works

Harvest House Publishers has made every effort to trace the ownership of all poems and quotes. In the event of a question arising from the use of a poem or quote, we regret any error made and will be pleased to make the necessary correction in future editions of this book.

Scripture quotations are taken from The Living Bible, Copyright © 1971 owned by assignment by Illinois Bank N.A. (as trustee). Used by permission of Tyndale House Publishers, Inc., Wheaton, Illinois 60189. All rights reserved; from the Holy Bible, New International Version®, Copyright © 1973, 1978, 1984 by the International Bible Society. Used by permission of Zondervan Publishing House; and from the New King James Version, Copyright © 1979, 1980, 1982 by Thomas Nelson, Inc., Publishers. Used by permission.

Printed in China.

00 01 02 03 04 05 06 07 08 09 / PP / 10 9 8 7 6 5 4 3 2

My heart is singing for joy...The light of understanding has shone in my little pupil's mind, and behold, all things are changed.

ANNE SULLIVAN

A teacher affects
eternity; he can
never tell where his
influence stops.

HENRY ADAMS

4

The great teacher must
not only give the best that
is in his subject, but what
is even more important,
the best that is in himself.

HERMAN KELLY

Teaching is a partnership
with God. You are not
molding iron nor chiseling
marble; you are working
with the Creator of the
universe in shaping
human character and
determining destiny.

RUTH VAUGHN

6

A professor can never better
distinguish himself in his
work than by encouraging
a clever pupil, for the true
discoverers are among them,
as comets amongst the stars.

LINNAEUS

7

Good teaching is one-fourth preparation and three-fourths theater.

GAIL GOODWIN

You can teach a student a lesson for a
day; but if you can teach him to learn by
creating curiosity, he will continue the
learning process as long as he lives.

CLAY P. BEDFORD

The entire object of true
education, is to make people
not merely do the right thing,
but to enjoy right things; not
merely industrious, but to love
industry; not merely learned,
but to love knowledge.

JOHN RUSKIN

A hundred years from now it will not matter...

what my bank account was,

the sort of house I lived in,

or the kind of car I drove.

But the world may be different

because I was important

in the life of a child.

AUTHOR UNKNOWN

A builder builded a temple,
He wrought it with grace and skill;
Pillars and groins and arches
All fashioned to work his will.
Men said, as they saw its beauty,
"It shall never know decay;
Great is thy skill, O Builder!
Thy fame shall endure for aye."

12

A teacher builded a temple
With loving and infinite care,
Planning each arch with patience,
Laying each stone with prayer.
None praised her unceasing efforts,
None knew of her wondrous plan,
For the temple the teacher builded
Was unseen by the eyes of man.

Gone is the Builder's temple,
Crumbled into the dust;
Low lies each stately pillar,
Food for consuming rust.
But the temple the Teacher builded
Will last while the ages roll,
For that beautiful, unseen temple
Was a child's immortal soul.

AUTHOR UNKNOWN

13

It is the supreme art of the teacher to awaken
joy in creative expression and knowledge.

ALBERT EINSTEIN

I touch the future. I teach.

CHRISTA MCAULIFFE

A Teacher's Prayer

Lord,

Enable me to teach with *wisdom,*
for I help to shape the mind.
Equip me to teach with *truth,*
for I help to shape the conscience.
Encourage me to teach with *vision,*
for I help to shape the future.
Empower me to teach with *love,*
for I help to shape the world.

AUTHOR UNKNOWN

Teachers, I believe, are the most
responsible and important
members of society because
their professional efforts affect
the fate of the earth.

HELEN CALDICOTT

The dream begins, most of the time,
with a teacher who believes in you,
who tugs and pushes and leads you on
to the next plateau, sometimes poking
you with a sharp stick called truth.

DAN RATHER

Teachers teach because they care. Teaching
young people is what they do best. It
requires long hours, patience, and care.

HORACE MANN

18

The art of teaching is the art
of assisting discovery.

MARK VAN DOREN

Better than a thousand days of diligent
study is one day with a great teacher.

PROVERB

Aa Bb Cc Dd

The whole art of teaching is only
the art of awakening the natural
curiosity of young minds for the
purpose of satisfying it afterwards.

ANATOLE FRANCE

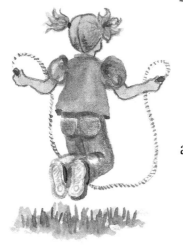

Whoever first coined the phrase "you're the wind beneath my wings" most assuredly was reflecting on the sublime influence of a very special teacher.

FRANK TRUJILLO

To waken interest and kindle enthusiasm is the sure way to teach easily and successfully.

TYRON EDWARDS

Education is not filling a
bucket, but lighting a fire.

WILLIAM YEATS

23

ABC · 123

A man's mind, stretched by
new ideas, can never go back
to its original dimensions.

OLIVER WENDELL HOLMES

It is better to ask some
of the questions than
know all of the answers.

JAMES THURBER

The happiest person is the person who thinks the most interesting thoughts.

TIMOTHY DWIGHT

Learning is an ornament in
prosperity, a refuge in adversity,
and a provision in old age.

ARISTOTLE

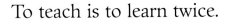

To teach is to learn twice.

JOSEPH JOUBERT

I am not a teacher, but an awakener.

ROBERT FROST

I am incurably convinced that the object of opening the mind, as of opening the mouth, is to shut it again on something solid.

G.K. CHESTERTON

If a teacher influences
but one, his influence
never stops.

AUTHOR UNKNOWN

He that governs well, leads
the blind...But he that
teaches, gives them eyes.

DAVID O. MCKAY

I have come to believe that a great teacher is a great artist and that there are as few as there are any other great artists. Teaching might even be the greatest of the arts since the medium is the human mind and spirit...

JOHN STEINBECK

In a completely rational society, the best of us would be teachers and the rest of us would have to settle for something else.

LEE IACCOCA

One looks back with appreciation to the
brilliant teachers, but with gratitude to
those who touched our human feelings.

CARL JUNG

What nobler employment, or more valuable to the state, than that of the man who instructs the rising generation?

CICERO

A word as to the
education of the heart.
We don't believe that
this can be imparted
through books; it can
only be imparted
through the loving
touch of the teacher.

AUTHOR UNKNOWN

Teaching is the greatest
act of optimism.

COLLEEN WILCOX

A wise teacher makes
learning a joy.

THE BOOK OF PROVERBS

Inspired teachers...cannot be
ordered by the gross from
the factory. They must be
discovered one by one.

JOHN JAY CHAPMAN

A teacher can never really *teach* unless he is still learning himself. A lamp can never light another lamp unless it continues to burn its own flame.

AUTHOR UNKNOWN

To be able to be caught
up into the world of
thought—that is being
educated.

EDITH HAMILTON

40

What sculpture is to a
block of marble, education
is to a human soul.

JOSEPH ADDISON

No man can be a good teacher
unless he has feelings of
warm affection toward his
pupils and a genuine desire
to impart to them what he
himself believes to be of value.

BERTRAND RUSSELL

It's not what is poured into a student
that counts, but what is planted.

LINDA CONWAY

Laurence Houseman once said, "A saint is one who makes goodness attractive." Surely, a great teacher does the same thing for education.

JOHN TRIMBLE

44

The task of the excellent teacher is to stimulate
"apparently ordinary" people to unusual effort.

PAT CROSS

The teacher, whether mother,
priest, or schoolmaster, is the
real maker of history.

H.G. WELLS

We should so live and labor in our time that what comes to us as seed may go to the next generation as blossom, and what came to us as blossom may go to them as fruit.

AUTHOR UNKNOWN

When love and skill work together,

expect a masterpiece.

JOHN RUSKIN

The secret of teaching is to
appear to have known all
your life what you learned
this afternoon.

AUTHOR UNKNOWN

Child, take my hand so that
I might walk in the shadow
of your faith in me.

AUTHOR UNKNOWN

Aa Bb Cc Dd

The man who can make hard
things easy is the educator.

RALPH WALDO EMERSON

The teacher is one who
makes two ideas grow
where only one grew before.

ELBERT HUBBARD

Nine-tenths of education
is encouragement.

ANATOLE FRANCE

He has put in his heart
the ability to teach...

THE BOOK OF EXODUS

The task of the modern
educator is not to cut
down jungles, but to
irrigate deserts.

C.S. LEWIS

Teachers can change lives
with just the right mix of
chalk and challenges.

JOYCE A. MYERS

Teaching is an instinctual
art, mindful of potential,
craving of realizations, a
pausing, seamless process.

A. BARTLETT GIAMATTI

Teaching is the royal road to learning.

JESSAMYN WEST

No bubble is so iridescent or
floats longer than that blown
by the successful teacher.

WILLIAM OSLER

The good teacher...discovers the natural gifts of his pupils and liberates them by the stimulating influence of the inspiration that he can impart.

STEPHEN NEILL

Those that know, do. Those that understand, teach.

ARISTOTLE

A good teacher is one who helps you become who you feel yourself to be.

JULIUS LESTER

If you cannot teach me to
fly, teach me to sing.

SIR JAMES BARRIE

And gladly would he learn,
and gladly teach.

GEOFFREY CHAUCER
THE CANTERBURY TALES

We find greatest joy, not in getting, but in expressing what we are...Men do not really live for honors or for pay; their gladness is not the taking and holding, but in doing, the striving, the building, the living. It is a higher joy to teach than to be taught.

R.J. BAUGHAN

ABC · 123

Teach us to number our
days aright, that we may
gain a heart of wisdom.

THE BOOK OF PSALMS

In seed time learn,
in harvest teach,
in winter enjoy.

WILLIAM BLAKE